SKYSCRAPER

Editorial: Steve Parker
Design: David West
                   Children's Book Design
Picture research: Cecilia Weston-Baker
Consultant: Stephen Vary (Structural Engineer)

Created and designed by
N.W. Books
70 Old Compton Street
London W1

First published in the
United States in 1988
Gloucester Press
387 Park Avenue South
New York, NY 10016

ISBN 0-531-17074-8

Library of Congress Catalog
Card Number: 87-82892

J721.042
OST

1. Skyscrapers
2. Architecture

Contents

ENGINEERS AT WORK

SKYSCRAPER

TIM OSTLER

GLOUCESTER PRESS

New York · London · Toronto · Sydney

WHY BUILD HIGH?

In our modern world, engineering and technology are becoming more and more complex. Researchers develop new steels, concretes, plastics and other materials. Architects and designers devise new ways of using them, while keeping up with changing fashions. Computers and their operators are vital. To stay in business, each company must try to keep ahead of its competitors.

At the center of design and construction are the engineers. Their work today will solve the problems posed by tomorrow's giant machines and great buildings, from airliners to oil rigs, power stations, highways, bridges, tunnels, cars – and skyscrapers. Why do we need such tall buildings? One reason is the sky-high cost of land in city centers, which often makes it more economical to build upward rather than outward. Also, many large companies find it efficient to have all their staff in one building, within easy reach of each other. And big business tends to see the skyscraper as a symbol of prestige. People imagine that the higher the skyscraper, the more successful the company it houses.

New York's tall buildings soar skyward. This city has more skyscrapers than any other, concentrated on the island of Manhattan.

Today's "mixed-use" building has offices, stores, apartments, even a restaurant at the top! However, most skyscrapers are almost entirely office space, owned by one company and perhaps rented to several others.

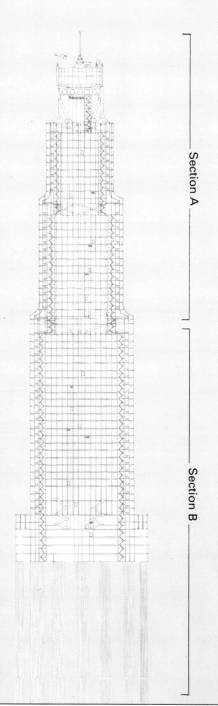

Section A

Section B

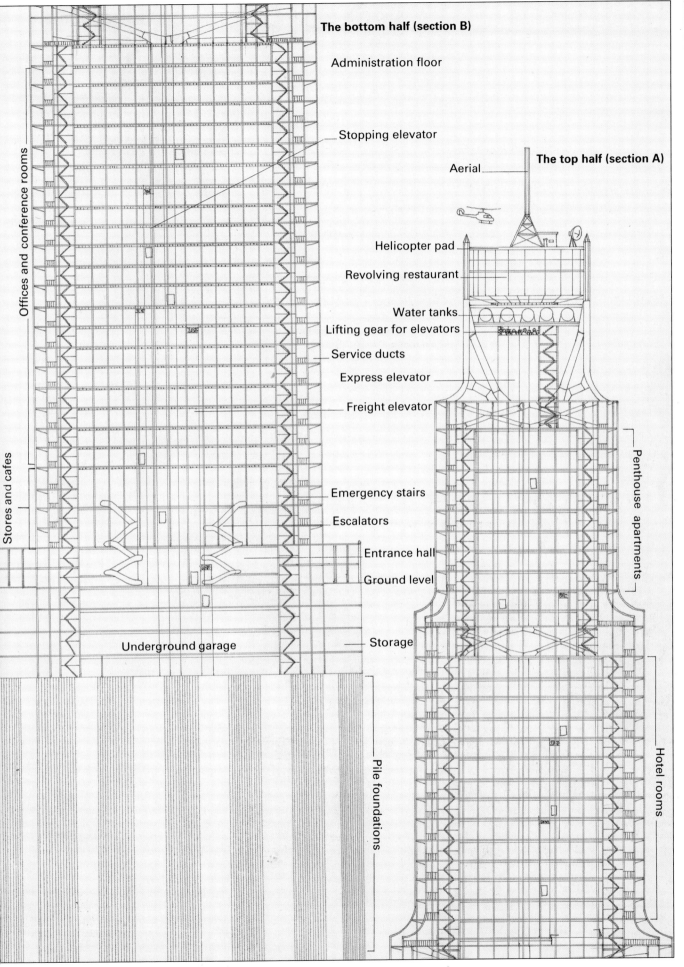

The bottom half (section B)

Administration floor

Stopping elevator

Aerial

The top half (section A)

Helicopter pad

Revolving restaurant

Water tanks

Lifting gear for elevators

Service ducts

Express elevator

Freight elevator

Emergency stairs

Escalators

Entrance hall

Ground level

Storage

Underground garage

Offices and conference rooms

Stores and cafes

Pile foundations

Penthouse apartments

Hotel rooms

DREAM IN THE SKY

Where does a skyscraper begin? An individual skyscraper often starts with the developer. He or she may have spent several years buying up adjacent sites in a city center, with the aim of acquiring one large site suitable for a giant building. Real estate experts advise the developer when likely sites come on the market, and geotechnical engineers are called in to check that the soil and rock will be able to take the weight of a tall building.

There will eventually be clients who buy or rent space in the building and fill it with people and equipment. Most skyscrapers are occupied by big companies, in businesses such as banking, insurance, oil, chemicals, computers or retailing. They may outgrow their old headquarters or they may merge with another company.

There are many other questions to consider. Will the people who occupy the building be able to travel there easily? Will the local supplies of electricity, water and drainage be sufficient? And will the city government allow such a mammoth building in its midst?

Once a possible area has been pinpointed, the developer may arrange an aerial survey by a light airplane or helicopter. The investors who put up the money, the clients who will use the building, and the staff from the city planning department can be flown over the site to see how the skyscraper will fit into its surroundings.

Before demolition begins, surveyors and engineers move in to check the suitability of the site. Here a surveyor uses a "dumpy level" to measure the slope of the ground. On a very large site, he could spend most of the day walking around. So engineers have developed the "laser level," which can check big areas for flatness. Long distances are measured by an "infrared" or "ultrasonic" tape measure, using infrared light or ultrasonic sound, and detecting the reflections.

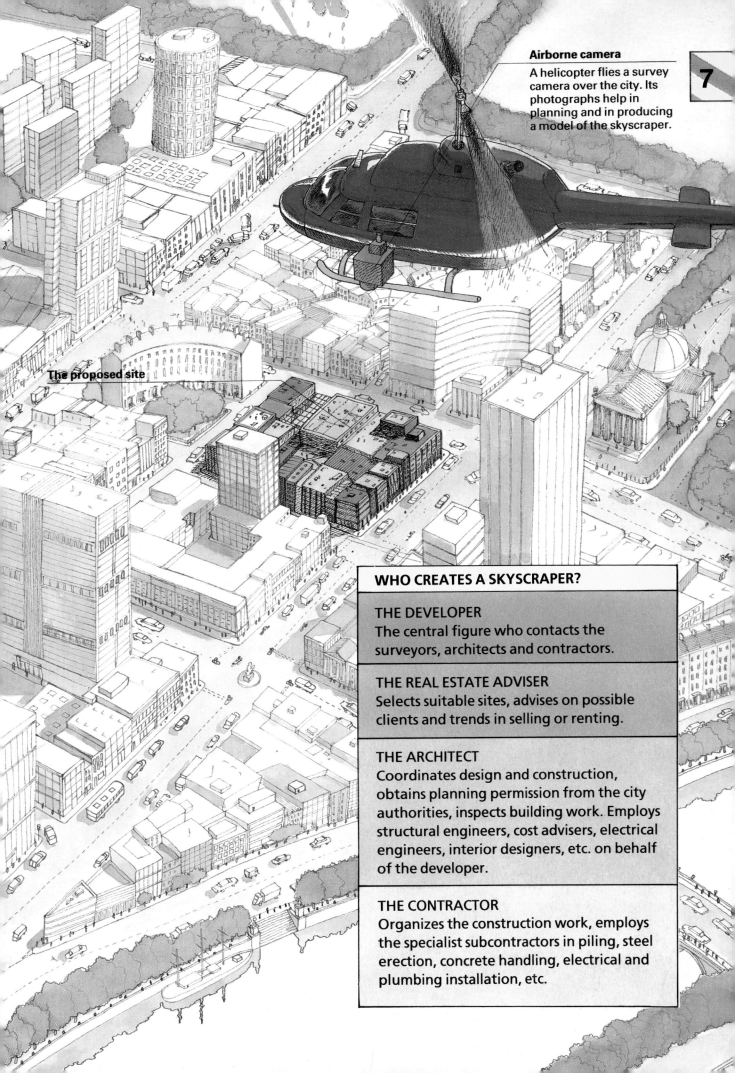

Airborne camera
A helicopter flies a survey camera over the city. Its photographs help in planning and in producing a model of the skyscraper.

The proposed site

WHO CREATES A SKYSCRAPER?

THE DEVELOPER
The central figure who contacts the surveyors, architects and contractors.

THE REAL ESTATE ADVISER
Selects suitable sites, advises on possible clients and trends in selling or renting.

THE ARCHITECT
Coordinates design and construction, obtains planning permission from the city authorities, inspects building work. Employs structural engineers, cost advisers, electrical engineers, interior designers, etc. on behalf of the developer.

THE CONTRACTOR
Organizes the construction work, employs the specialist subcontractors in piling, steel erection, concrete handling, electrical and plumbing installation, etc.

THE ARCHITECTS

The overall shape and character of a skyscraper may be the brainchild of one person. But the complete design, from the deepest foundations to the height of the aerial, is an enormously complicated job. The chief architect heads a team of perhaps 30 assistants, each responsible for one aspect of the building at a certain stage during its design and construction.

The architects call on many experts. Structural engineers advise on the supporting framework, whether it should be made of steel girders or reinforced concrete, and how safe and economical it will be to construct. Mechanical and electrical engineers face the problem of making the building habitable. Will there be enough light and circulating air? What about noise levels and warmth? Will people have sufficient water supplies and be able to board an elevator quickly? About 16,000 people work in the world's tallest skyscraper, Chicago's Sears Building; thousands more visit each day.

The Hong Kong and Shanghai Bank Building, in Hong Kong, had a local culture consultant. He advised on *Feng-shui*, the ancient Chinese art of placing a building in the landscape so that it could not be affected by evil spirits and dragons hiding behind nearby hills.

The skyscraper takes shape in the architect's sketches (right). As detailed work begins, designers use CAD (Computer-Aided Design, far right) to help them devise, for example, a floor structure that can be repeated for most of the stories. Computer plotters draw up the plans (below right). A model of the Hong Kong and Shanghai Bank, riddled with pressure sensors, is tested in a wind tunnel (below). The model city mimics airflow around the building.

DESIGNS FOR SKELETONS OF TALL BUILDINGS

Steel girders form the framework of most skyscrapers. But the strength of the steel skeleton depends on the way the girders are arranged. Shown here are designs which are generally the most economical for buildings of certain heights, from small to very tall. The belt truss version gains strength from the triangulated (trussed) belts half way up and at the top. The framed tube has no strong central column but an outer skin of girders at right angles. The bundled-tubes design, used in the Sears Building, consists of several square tubes joined together.

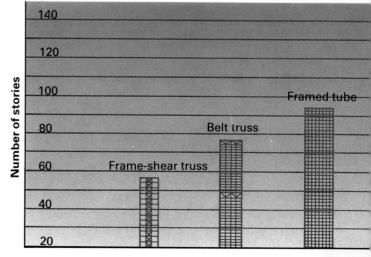

Number of stories

140
120
100
80
60
40
20

Frame-shear truss

Belt truss

Framed tube

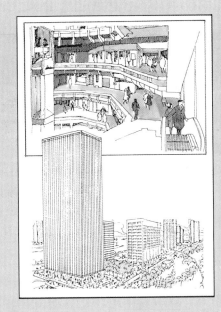

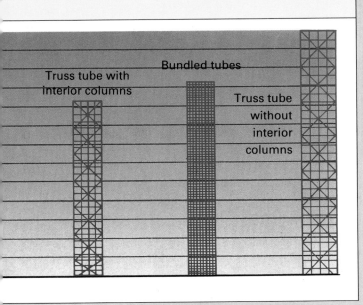

Truss tube with interior columns

Bundled tubes

Truss tube without interior columns

THE UNDERGROUND MAZE

Under a typical city street runs a spaghetti-like tangle of water pipes, drains, sewers, gas mains, electricity cables and phone lines. Engineers must work with city staff to plan the best way of tapping in to these local services, to provide supplies for the skyscraper. Sometimes new services must be laid, causing work many streets away.

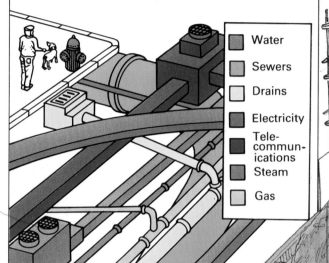

■	Water
■	Sewers
□	Drains
■	Electricity
■	Tele-communications
■	Steam
□	Gas

Ball and crane

Older brick built structures, which are relatively small and weak, can be demolished by a heavy ball swung on the cable of a crane. Leaning walls and chimneys may need to be helped down carefully with crowbars. Once the area is safe, the rubble can be trucked away.

Pipes and cables

Great care is taken to detect water mains, electricity cables and other services, and to seal them off as necessary.

Site offices

The contractors mastermind the operation from portable cabins. As the skyscraper grows, so do these offices.

Holding up the hole

A retaining wall of corrugated metal sheet (sheet pile wall) holds up the sides of the great hole.

Construction starts with destruction. As one part of the site is being cleared, digging for foundations takes place in another part.

Rubble removal

Good quality rubble may be in demand elsewhere, to make "hardcore" (crushed brick and stone) for another building project.

Digging deep

Excavators dig into softer soil, loading it into a conveyor-belt line of trucks. Rock must first be broken up by pneumatic drills or explosives.

When the contractors receive the final go-ahead, work can start on clearing the site. Old buildings must be pulled down and their remains taken away. Then diggers and dump trucks move in to excavate the foundations. A continuous line of trucks removes mud, soil and rock, probably to a landfill site in the area. There can be no delay, because when so many large machines are in use, time costs a lot of money.

The architects and engineers check various plans of the site. They visit the city authorities, the electrical and water companies, and several other organizations. They must locate the main services and ensure that their work does not disrupt supplies to local people.

Surveyors and engineers come onto the site, to measure distances and depths and to check the nature of the subsoil. Water may seep through the soil into the pit being dug, and this has to be pumped away. Geotechnical engineers estimate whether the water seepage could affect foundations of nearby buildings, causing the ground to dry, crack or even subside.

Carefully placed explosive charges cause a tall building to collapse in on itself without damaging adjacent buildings.

BEGIN AT THE BOTTOM

A skyscraper presents the structural engineer with two special problems. First is weight. The Empire State Building weighs nearly 400,000 tons. To prevent such a structure sinking into the ground, foundations must be massive. They usually take the form of piles – long columns of concrete or steel stretching deep into the earth. In New York, home of the Empire State Building, this problem is not too great since solid bedrock is close to the surface. London rests on clay, and piles must go much deeper. The main foundations of London's National Westminster Tower extend 59 feet below the ground, and 375 piles were driven down a further 78 feet.

The second problem is wind. A gentle breeze on the ground may be a gale many stories up. On a very windy day, one of New York's two 110-story World Trade Center towers is being pushed sideways with a total force of 13,000 tons. This force must be transmitted by the structure to the foundations, which have to be strong enough to stop the whole building toppling over, like a tree torn out by its roots in a gale.

Basement walls

The top of the finished pile (4) may be used to support the temporary retaining wall (5). Concrete, usually poured onto reinforcing metal rods (reinforced concrete) is used to form the walls of the sub-basements and basements (6).

Once the site is cleared to the correct depth, construction can start. Piles are made and a reinforced concrete raft is laid down to form the base of the skyscraper.

Putting in piles

On the cleared site, the holes for the piles are drilled and an outer casing installed (1). A large H-section girder is centered in the hole (2), and ready-mixed concrete from a fleet of mixer trucks is poured in (3).

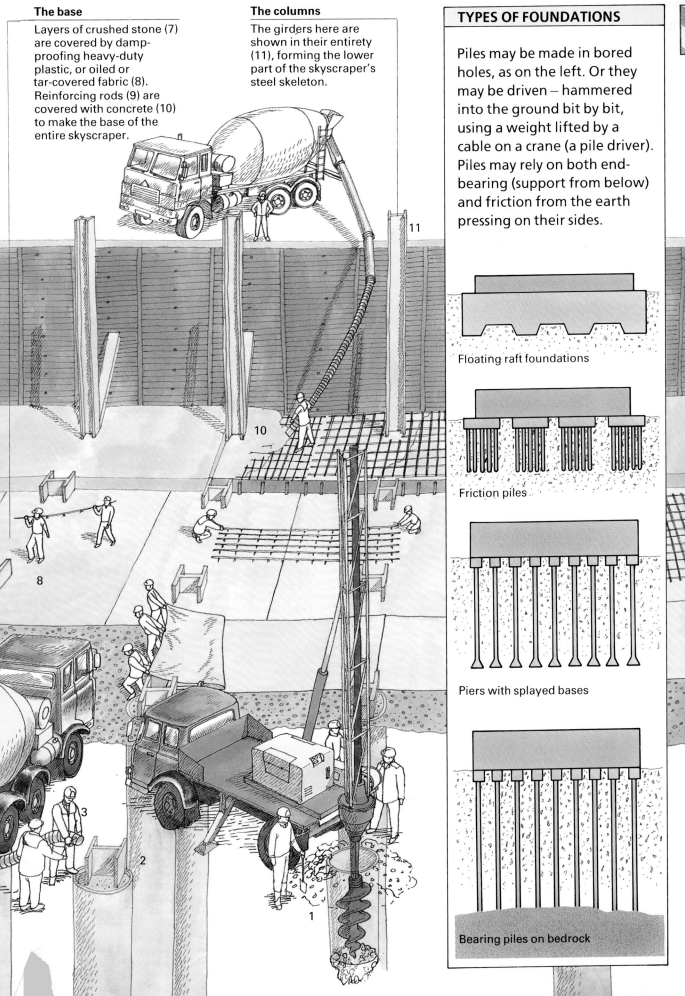

The base

Layers of crushed stone (7) are covered by damp-proofing heavy-duty plastic, or oiled or tar-covered fabric (8). Reinforcing rods (9) are covered with concrete (10) to make the base of the entire skyscraper.

The columns

The girders here are shown in their entirety (11), forming the lower part of the skyscraper's steel skeleton.

TYPES OF FOUNDATIONS

Piles may be made in bored holes, as on the left. Or they may be driven — hammered into the ground bit by bit, using a weight lifted by a cable on a crane (a pile driver). Piles may rely on both end-bearing (support from below) and friction from the earth pressing on their sides.

Floating raft foundations

Friction piles

Piers with splayed bases

Bearing piles on bedrock

CRANES AND ACCESS

City centers are not the easiest of places to move around. The planners and engineers building a skyscraper are faced with enormous problems of access. To build the National Westminster Tower, 100,000 tons of concrete and nearly 4,000 tons of structural steel had to be brought into the middle of London. Large prefabricated girders and ready-made sections are especially difficult to transport through narrow, traffic-filled city streets. There is little storage space on the site, so hauling contractors must deliver parts and materials as and when they are needed, often to the exact hour.

In some cases, it is necessary for the developer to buy up a neighboring building and demolish it, to make room for storage and maneuvering large parts. The cost is minimal compared to the millions spent on the main skyscraper.

Soon, tower cranes begin to sprout on the site. They grow above the building as they lift materials and machinery to great heights. Their operators keep in touch with workers on the ground by radio-telephone.

Large parts are often delivered at night to avoid traffic. Above right, a preconstructed section (made in West Germany) arrives for Paris's Pompidou Center. Below right, cranes work through the night to keep on schedule. In the main photograph, a tower crane lifts materials from a delivery truck onto the site. Arranging the crane's daily workload is an intricate job in itself.

THE TOWER CRANE

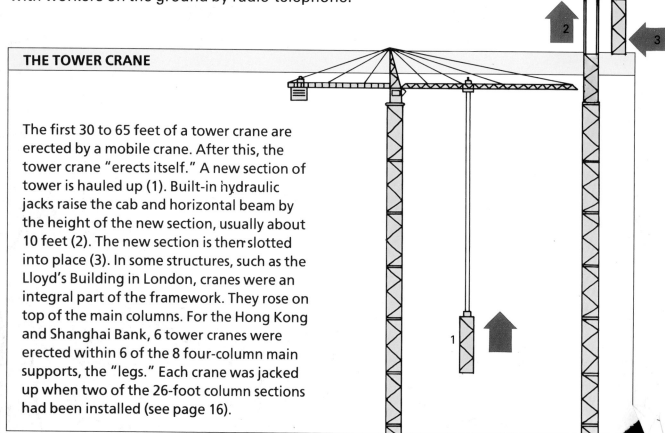

The first 30 to 65 feet of a tower crane are erected by a mobile crane. After this, the tower crane "erects itself." A new section of tower is hauled up (1). Built-in hydraulic jacks raise the cab and horizontal beam by the height of the new section, usually about 10 feet (2). The new section is then slotted into place (3). In some structures, such as the Lloyd's Building in London, cranes were an integral part of the framework. They rose on top of the main columns. For the Hong Kong and Shanghai Bank, 6 tower cranes were erected within 6 of the 8 four-column main supports, the "legs." Each crane was jacked up when two of the 26-foot column sections had been installed (see page 16).

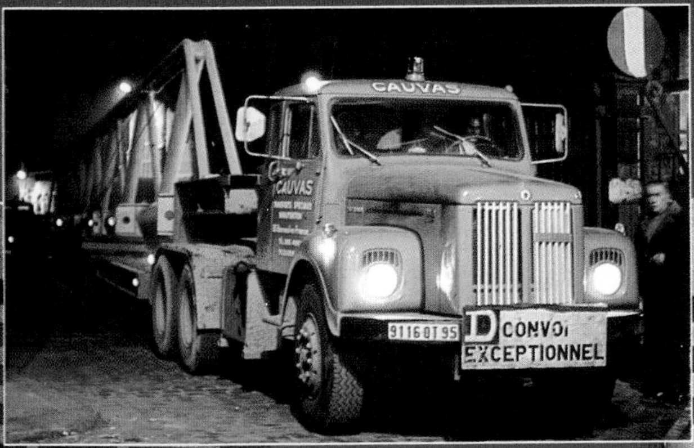
CAUVAS
CONVOI
EXCEPTIONNEL

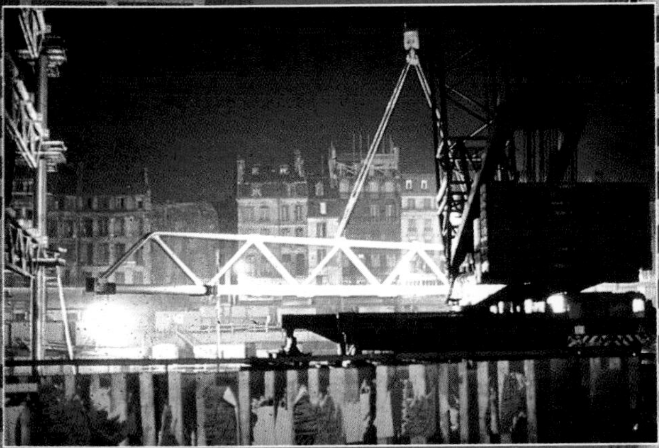

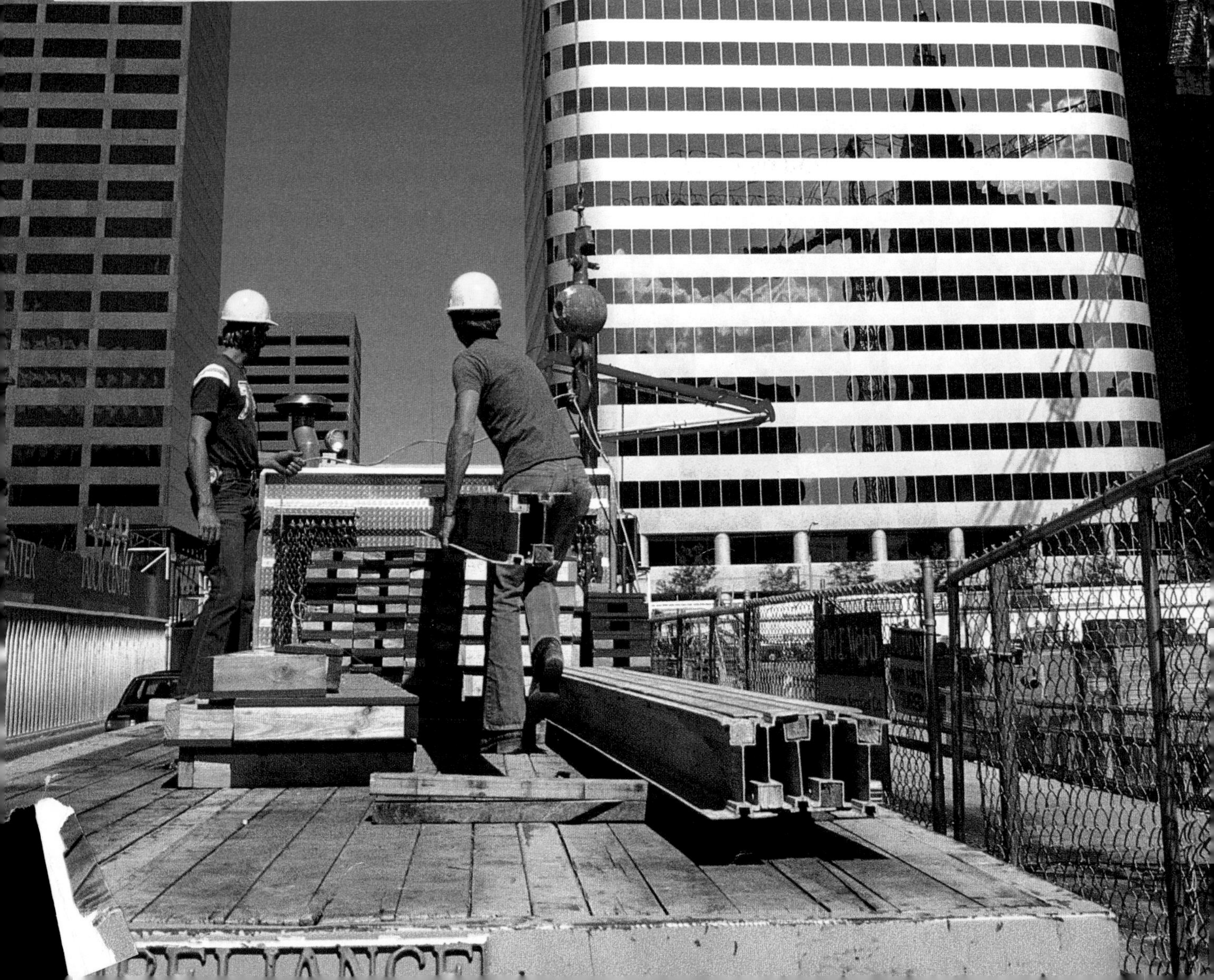

THE STEEL SKELETON

Most modern skyscrapers have a framework made of steel. The Sears Building in Chicago has nearly 80,000 tons of it (along with 183,000 cubic feet of concrete). In some buildings it is clearly visible. For example, the John Hancock Center in Chicago has enormous diagonal steel girders ("truss" design) that brace the framework against the wind. In other tall buildings the girders are hidden behind the walls. The steel skeleton supports the external and internal walls, the floors, and all other major parts.

One problem with steel is that, in the temperature of a fire, it loses its "temper" and so its strength. So the steel parts of the framework must be protected against fire. One way is to wrap them in heat-resistant cases made of mineral fibers. Another is to spray them with a fireproof substance that expands and then sets hard. A third way is to design the steel pieces as tubes and fill them with water which circulates and cools the steel in the event of a fire. The Pompidou Center supporting beams use this method.

Steel erectors and engineers spend their working day dozens of stories above the ground. Safety is vital at such heights, with heavy steel beams swinging in the wind. When finished, the top of the skyscraper may sway up to a yard with the wind.

Cranes on top of each leg of the Hong Kong and Shanghai Bank lift materials around the site. Giant 110-foot beams are suspended between the legs. The 25,000 tons of steel in the framework were made in England and shipped halfway around the world to Hong Kong.

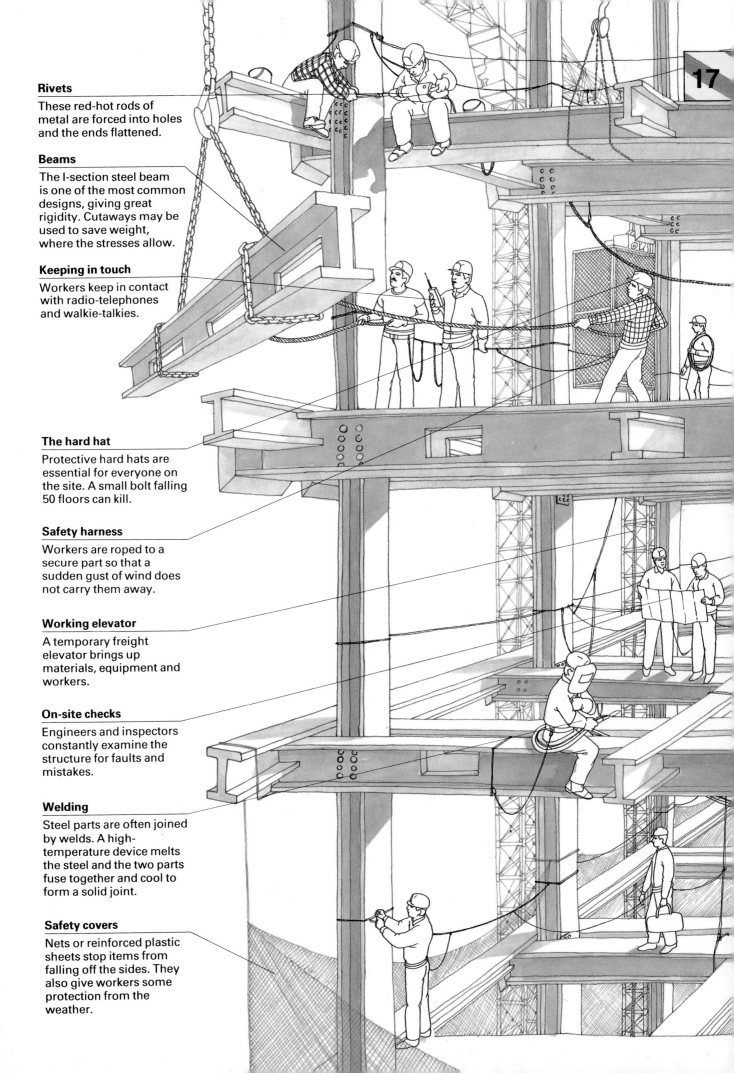

Rivets

These red-hot rods of metal are forced into holes and the ends flattened.

Beams

The I-section steel beam is one of the most common designs, giving great rigidity. Cutaways may be used to save weight, where the stresses allow.

Keeping in touch

Workers keep in contact with radio-telephones and walkie-talkies.

The hard hat

Protective hard hats are essential for everyone on the site. A small bolt falling 50 floors can kill.

Safety harness

Workers are roped to a secure part so that a sudden gust of wind does not carry them away.

Working elevator

A temporary freight elevator brings up materials, equipment and workers.

On-site checks

Engineers and inspectors constantly examine the structure for faults and mistakes.

Welding

Steel parts are often joined by welds. A high-temperature device melts the steel and the two parts fuse together and cool to form a solid joint.

Safety covers

Nets or reinforced plastic sheets stop items from falling off the sides. They also give workers some protection from the weather.

ADDING THE CLADDING

If the steel framework is the "bones" of a skyscraper, then the cladding is its "skin." On a tall building the walls and floors have nothing to do with the structure – they simply hang from or sit on the framework.

The external walls present a major problem, since they take the full force of the weather. Wind buffets the panels, rain hits them horizontally, ice forms in the cracks in winter, and the hot sun makes them expand in summer. Different materials expand at different rates. Equivalent coefficients of expansion (a measure of the rate of

The skyscraper is now ready to receive its floors and external walls. As soon as the weather is shut out, work on the internal walls and services can begin. Teams of fitters and engineers make their way upward, completing their tasks story by story.

Many skyscrapers have "curtain walls" on the outside. The wall panels are made in a factory, taken by truck to the site, and lifted into place by a crane. They hang from the steel girders on each floor, like curtains hang from a curtain rod.

expansion) are 90 for some plastics, 24 for aluminum, 17 for stainless steel, 12 for concrete and 9 for glass. So the engineer cannot mix materials on the outside without designing in special weatherproof expansion joints. Cladding materials include glass (for windows, of course), bronze or steel panels, very thin sheets of marble or granite, and silver-anodized aluminum. The fixings must be so secure that, even during the tremors of an earthquake, they cannot be shaken loose and crash to the street below.

Joints and seals

Joints must take up expansion and keep out wind, rain, dirt and noise. They must also allow slight movement, since any skyscraper sways a little in the wind and "breathes" with changes in temperature.

Panels

Factory-made cladding panels are positioned by crane and fixed in place.

Fireproofing

The steel beams and columns are covered with fire-resistant cladding, such as planks of mineral fibers in an aluminum foil casing.

Sprinkler system

One of the many safety features is the automatic sprinkler system, which sprays water if there is a fire.

Internal columns

These are fireproofed and eventually covered with panels to match the decor of the rooms inside.

Ceiling

Suspended ceilings are hung from the beams and floor formers.

Floor base

Floor bases are usually made of slabs of concrete reinforced with metal rods or strips.

Space for services

Between the ceiling of one story and the floor of the one above is a space perhaps a yard or more deep. This carries air-conditioning ducts, electrical cables, water pipes and many other services.

Floor formers

Some skyscrapers have floors made of corrugated metal sheeting laid over the steel beams.

False floor

The raised floor is fixed in place above the concrete floor base. The space below may carry computer cables and phone wires.

THE SERVICES

The services are the "life-blood" of the skyscraper, and the service ducts are its "arteries." The main services are electricity, water, gas, waste water disposal, sewage disposal, solid waste disposal, telecommunications (phone lines, optical fibers, computer networks and so on), some combination of heating, cooling and air-conditioning . . . added to these might be a public address system, alarms, sprinklers, smoke and heat and movement detectors for safety and security, a closed-circuit television system . . .

THE CENTRAL COLUMN

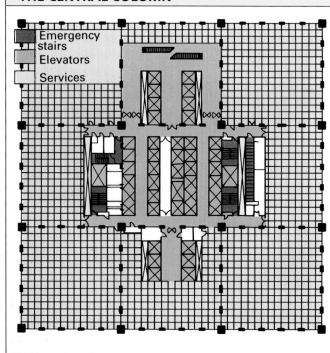

Emergency stairs
Elevators
Services

This is the plan of a Sky Lobby, on the 33rd floor of the Sears Building. The central square tube of the 9 tubes that make up the structure is entirely taken up by stopping elevators and service ducts. Express elevators (14 at this level) are above and below. To the left are the transformer room, main electrical supply and stairs; on the right are more stairs and that vital service – the toilet block! The surrounding spaces are taken up by office staff.

Designing and installing all these services and systems presents enormous problems of organization. The lower stories of the skyscraper may be carpeted, with their lights and fawcets working, while the upper stories are still only steel beams. The engineers must design and build the systems as self-contained modules. For instance, as one group of floors is completed, its electrical power can be switched in and the circuits checked without endangering the electricians working with bare wires on the floors above.

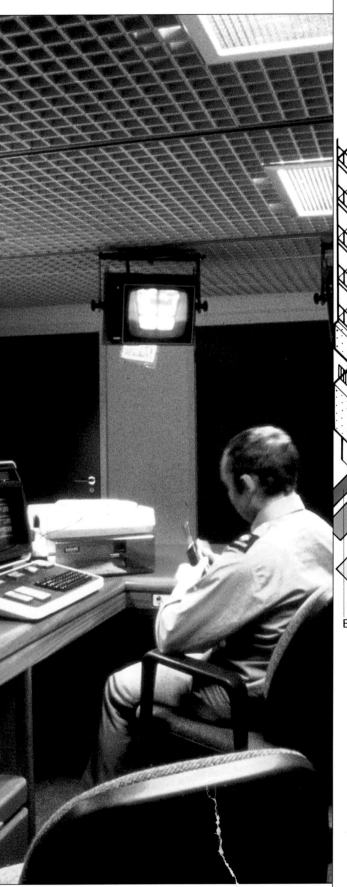

The building staff monitors services and security in the Lloyd's Building from the computerized control room.

THE SERVICE DUCT

Electrical power

Telecommunications

Water supply

Air-conditioning

Elevators

Drains and sewage

Telecommunications

Water supply

Electrical power

Drains and sewage

Usually, all supplies and systems are concentrated together in one large duct or tunnel. This makes maintenance and repair easier. It also means that engineers and other specialists called to make adjustments do not disrupt the occupants. In today's "intelligent building," computers keep track of the state of the services and warn when problems arise.

UPS AND DOWNS

Skyscrapers would not be possible without elevators. Goods hoists have been around for centuries, lifting materials (and sometimes people). But the great problem was safety: how could disaster be prevented if the cable snapped? In 1852, the engineer Elisha Otis designed the first safety elevator, with guide rails on each side of the shaft. If something went wrong, spring-loaded cams automatically gripped the rails and held the car firmly. In 1857, Otis installed the first safety passenger elevator in a New York store.

Today, elevators come in many shapes and sizes. Express elevators stop at only a few floors, usually near the ground and at the top. Stopping or commuter elevators go to all floors. The Sears Building has 102 high-speed elevators, including 14 double-deckers. There are also freight and service elevators, and emergency elevators for security staff, firemen and so on.

Modern elevators move at amazing speeds, more than 1,650 feet per minute. The limits are not technical, but human – above these speeds, people feel dizzy and sick.

The two main types of elevator are cable-operated (right) and hydraulic (far right). The hydraulic version works on the same engineering principle as a hydraulic car jack. The elevator car is pushed upward from below by pressurized oil in a series of telescopic pistons. This type is used for smaller buildings and moves at a slower speed than the cable-operated type.

Escalators or moving staircases are midway between stairs and elevators. They are useful for short journeys of only a few floors. These escalators are in the Lloyd's Building in London. From them are breathtaking views over the enormous central hall, or atrium, of the building. The atrium lets in daylight through its curved glass roof so that offices inside have some natural lighting.

Control gear

Nowadays the "intelligent elevator" is computer-controlled. The computer works out the most economical journey for each car, depending on how many people are waiting on each floor.

Lifting motor

An electric motor winches the car up and down on a steel cable. In a stopping elevator the motor is geared down. In a high-speed elevator the motor shaft may drive the winch pulley directly.

Main cable

Engineers service all parts regularly and inspect the cable for kinks or fraying.

Guide rails

These prevent the car swaying, and they are gripped by the safety cams in the event of cable or motor failure.

Elevator car

Large elevators can carry 20 people or more – a load of perhaps 3,000 lbs (1.5 tons).

Call button

Safety brake

The cams automatically grip the guide rails if there is trouble.

Counterweight and tracks

Concrete or cast-iron weights on the other end of the main cable balance the weight of the elevator car.

Floor buffer

Hydraulic piston

Oil pumped into the telescopic pistons raises the car.

Oil pump and reservoir

A valve drains oil from the pistons into the reservoir, to lower the car.

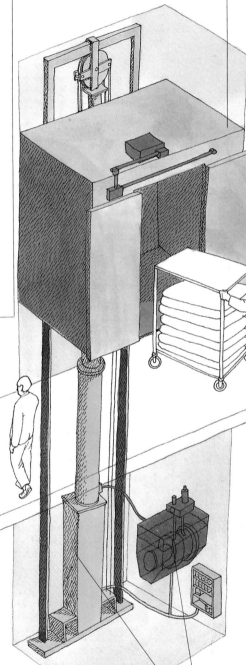

COMING ALIVE!

At last, the skyscraper comes alive. The main construction work is finished. At the opening ceremony, the company chiefs declare the building completed. Workers and visitors throng the offices and stores, and life settles into a daily routine.

But the engineer's work is never finished. There are thousands of parts and pieces of equipment that need constant checking, maintenance, service and repair, from elevators and air-conditioning plants to the red flashing lights on top that warn aircraft. The needs of the occupants may change, and the engineers discuss with interior designers the best way to replan an office and move the internal walls, lights and computer cables.

Many of the daily tasks will be designed into the building, so that they can be carried out smoothly and without disturbance. Mail arrives, food and drinks are delivered, stationery and washroom supplies need renewing, garbage is sent down chutes and taken away in huge dumpsters, and cleaning staff come in at night to wash, vacuum and clean. The skyscraper lives on .

The newly opened skyscraper towers above the city center, proud symbol of the art of the architect and of the engineer's science. Its stepped-back design, with stories becoming smaller with height, lets the maximum daylight reach the ground. It also prevents too much shading of nearby buildings.

The Lloyd's Building is "inside out" – it has many of its pipes and ducts on the outside. Permanent cranes on top of the main columns lift replacement parts into place. Clearly visible is the curved glass roof of the atrium, the central hall.

External maintenance

City air is often dusty and polluted. The outside of the skyscraper must be cleaned regularly, or the daylight let in by the windows is reduced. Small cranes on rails around the top of the building lower workers in gondolas, who clean and check the cladding panels, joints and seals.

Administration

The administration staff must keep track of everything entering and leaving the building to ensure its smooth running. They deal with all aspects, from food to a banquet in the penthouse to toilet paper for the dozens of washrooms.

Security

In our modern world, security is an ever-present worry. Staff patrol the corridors day and night, looking for suspicious packages or people. Closed-circuit television watches public spaces such as the shopping malls.

Waste disposal

The thousands of people in a large skyscraper generate tons of garbage each day. This is packed into huge dumpster bins and removed from the service bay with the minimum of fuss and unpleasant smells.

THE YOUNG ENGINEER

Skyscrapers have been around for less than a hundred years. They are among the biggest engineering projects ever undertaken. Yet they use some of the simplest engineering principles. Try the projects shown here, which demonstrate some of the basic scientific laws involved in designing and constructing a tall building.

Foundations

The foundations must support the weight of the skyscraper, and also resist the leverage caused by winds. A larger surface area can support more weight than a small one, as shown below. Press on a small coin placed in a tray of sand. It will push the grains out of the way and sink easily (1). Next, cut out a disk of stiff cardboard and put this under the coin, then press. The larger surface of the disk spreads the weight and prevents sinking (2). The concrete raft of a skyscraper works in the same way (page 13). Alternatively, cut some wooden sticks to length and push them into the sand to rest on the bottom of the tray, and place the coin on them (3). The sticks transfer the force pressing on the coin down to the solid base, just as bearing piles transfer the weight of the skyscraper to solid bedrock lying below the subsoil (page 13).

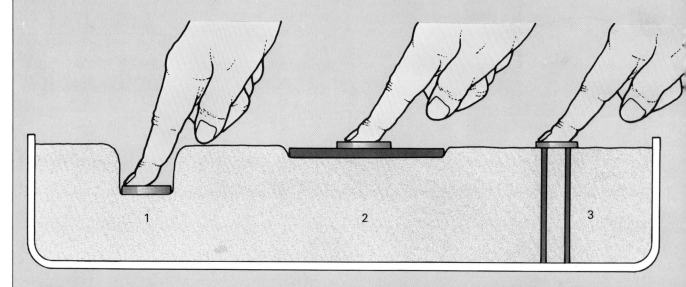

Curved for strength

Curved or arched designs can give great strength. An egg is easily broken by pressing on its flatter side (1), but not by pushing its pointed end (2). Arch supports use a similar principle. Place a sheet of thin cardboard on two supports, and it sags (3). Cut a curved support from a similar piece of cardboard and tape it in position, and the upper sheet should be firmly supported by this arch (4).

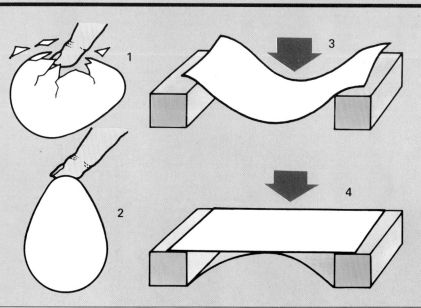

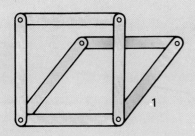

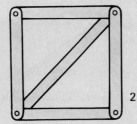

Strong triangles (above)

A square made from strips of cardboard joined by split pins is easily pushed out of shape (1). A diagonal brace or truss (2) makes it stronger. Many skyscrapers have trusses to stiffen their structure (page 8).

Ribs and beams (below)

Corrugated cardboard bends easily in one direction (1). Add cross-beams and it forms a firm platform (2), a principle used for the corrugated metal sheeting found in skyscraper floors (page 19).

The wind funnel

A skyscraper may create a "wind funnel" of its own when built. Make a model of city buildings with cardboard boxes. Tape pieces of thin folded paper to the "streets." Then mimic the wind blowing along the street using a hair-dryer (set on cold). The pieces of paper should bend slightly in the breeze (1). Next, place a model skyscraper in the middle, and blow again with the hair-dryer. Air squeezing past the skyscraper picks up speed and bends the pieces of paper much more (2). This means a troublesome gale at street level (page 8).

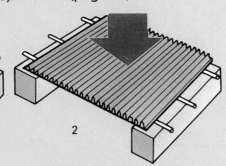

Swaying in the wind

Skyscrapers are built with "give" in their structure, so that they sway in high winds. But it becomes very dangerous if a tall building "resonates." This means it sways back and forth with a certain speed which equals the natural vibration speed of the structure. The wobbling then gets more and more violent, and the building may shake itself to pieces and fall down. You can show this by making a tall tube of thin cardboard and taping it down. Set a hair-dryer on cold and blow it at the tube. If the air speed is right, the tube may shake violently (page 12).

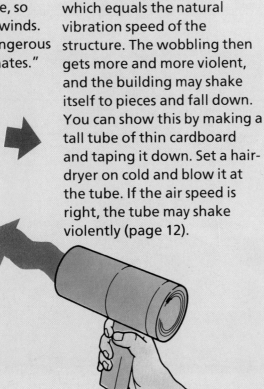

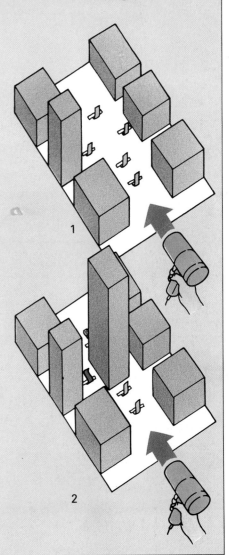

TALLEST SKYSCRAPERS

The world's Top 10 skyscrapers are all in the United States, and many others in the Top 100 are also. Why? Technically, it is possible to build a skyscraper almost anywhere. But engineering is only part of the story. Skyscrapers cost immense amounts of money, and usually only rich countries with multinational, big-profit corporations are likely to have them. Below are the world's tallest building (Sears) and the world's tallest apartment buildings (Lake Point), all in Chicago. Britain's tallest building (and Europe's second tallest) is the National Westminster Tower, at 610 feet. There are plans in several big cities to build skyscrapers up to 3,000 feet high. Yet another challenge for the engineers!

Building (City)	Year completed	No. of stories	Height m	(ft.)	Use
The 10 tallest					
Sears Building (Chicago)	1974	110	443	(1,454)	Office
World Trade Center (New York)	1972-3	110	412	(1,350)	Office
Empire State Building (New York)	1931	102	381	(1,250)	Office
Standard Oil (Chicago)	1973	80	346	(1,136)	Office
John Hancock Center (Chicago)	1968	100	344	(1,127)	Multi
Chrysler Building (New York)	1930	77	319	(1,046)	Office
Texas Commerce Plaza (Houston)	1981	75	305	(1,002)	Office
Allied Bank Plaza (Houston)	1983	71	296	(970)	Office
American International (New York)	1931	66	290	(950)	Office
Columbia Center (Seattle)	1983	76	287	(940)	Office
Tallest skyscrapers outside the USA					
First Bank Tower (Toronto)	1975	72	285	(935)	Office
Palace of Culture (Warsaw)	1955	42	241	(790)	Office
MLC Center (Sydney)	1976	70	240	(786)	Office
Commerce Court West (Toronto)	1974	57	239	(784)	Office
Singapore Treasury (Singapore)	1986	52	235	(770)	Office
Tour Maine Montparnasse (Paris)	1973	64	229	(751)	Office
Sunshine 60 Building (Tokyo)	1978	60	226	(742)	Office
Raffles City Hotel (Singapore)	1986	70	226	(741)	Hotel
Dominion Bank Tower (Toronto)	1967	56	224	(736)	Office
Carlton Center (Johannesburg)	1973	50	220	(722)	Office
Shinjuku Center (Tokyo)	1979	54	216	(709)	Office
Hopewell Center (Hong Kong)	1980	65	216	(709)	Multi
Shinjuku Mitsui (Tokyo)	1974	55	212	(696)	Office
Shinjuku Nomura (Tokyo)	1978	53	210	(690)	Office
Overseas-Chinese Banking Corporation (Singapore)	1976	52	201	(660)	Office
Shinjuku Sumitomo (Tokyo)	1974	52	200	(656)	Office
Central Park Torre Oficinas (Caracas)	1979	56	200	(656)	Office
Ukraine Hotel (Moscow)	1961	34	198	(650)	Hotel

Lake Point Towers in Chicago

The Sears Building in Chicago

GLOSSARY

Air-conditioning Some combination of warming, cooling, drying and moistening (humidifying) the air in a building, to make it pleasant for people and suitable for delicate machinery.

Atrium A large open space or hallway in a building, usually several stories high.

Beam Horizontal part of a building's structure, usually made of steel.

CAD Computer-Aided Design, the use of computers in design, for example, to repeat the plan for a panel or a floor many times, automatically.

Cladding The outside walls of a skyscraper, usually made as panels and fixed to the structural frame.

Column Vertical part of a building's structure, usually made of steel or reinforced concrete, which transmits the weight of the skyscraper down to the foundations.

Concrete A mixture of cement, fine aggregate (sand), coarse aggregate (gravel or small stones) and water that sets hard.

Corrugated A flat sheet folded repeatedly into small U or V shaped channels to give strength in one direction.

Elevator A small room that travels up and down in a shaft and transports people and goods.

Foundations The base of a building that transmits its weight safely into the surrounding subsoil or rock and stops it sinking or leaning.

Geotechnical Concerned with the nature of soils and rocks and how they affect foundations and underground services.

Girder A beam, or column, or some other part of the structural frame.

Hydraulic Worked by fluid under pressure.

Piles Long, finger-like parts of the foundations, that spread a tall building's weight deep in the ground and stop it from toppling over.

Reinforced concrete Concrete that sets around metal rods, girders or meshes, to give it greater strength.

Resonance The swaying of a skyscraper back and forth in time with its natural period of vibration, so that the swaying gets more and more violent.

Services Electricity, water, drainage, gas and other supplies.

Skyscraper A tall building, usually with walls that hang from a structural steel frame rather than forming the structure themselves.

Steel Iron from a blast furnace that has had nearly all the carbon removed (down to 1.7 per cent or less) and small quantities of other substances added. There are many types of steel for specialized applications.

Story One level, or floor, of a building.

Telecommunications Electrical and/or optical fiber cables that carry the signals from telephones, computers and other electronic equipment.

Truss A diagonal brace on a frame, that forms triangles with the other parts and so gives great rigidity.

INDEX

Photographic Credits:
Cover and page 18: Tony Stone Assoc.; pages 4, 6, 9 (top and bottom) and 22: Art Directors; pages 9 (left) and 20-21: Ove Arup; page 11: Spectrum; page 16: Hutchison Library; page 24: Robert Harding Library; page 28 (left): Steve Parker; page 28 (right): J. Allen Cash.